P9-CMO-891

Creating and Implementing Your Strategic Plan

John M. Bryson

▪ ▪ ▪ ▪ ▪

Farnum K. Alston

Creating and Implementing Your Strategic Plan

A Workbook for Public and Nonprofit Organizations

Jossey-Bass Publishers ▪ San Francisco

Library of Congress Cataloging-in-Publication Data

Bryson, John M. (John Moore), date.
Creating and implementing your strategic plan : a workbook for public and nonprofit organizations / John M. Bryson, Farnum K. Alston.—1st ed.
p. cm.—(The Jossey-Bass public administration series) (The Jossey-Bass nonprofit sector series)
Includes bibliographical references and index.
ISBN 0-7879-0142-3
1. Strategic planning. 2. Nonprofit organizations—Management. 3. Public administration. I. Alston, Farnum K. II. Title. III. Series. IV. Series: The Jossey-Bass nonprofit sector series.
HD30.28.B788 1996
658.4'012—dc20 95-32628

FIRST EDITION
PB Printing 10 9 8 7 6 5 4 3 2 1

A joint publication in

The Jossey-Bass
Public Administration Series

and

The Jossey-Bass
Nonprofit Sector Series

Contents

Preface

Today, public and nonprofit organizations and many communities face a bewildering array of challenges, including the following:

- Significantly increased—or reduced—demands for their programs, services, and products
- More active and vocal employees and "clients"
- Heightened (sometimes staggering) uncertainty about the future
- Pressures to "reinvent" or "reengineer" themselves, to engage in Total Quality Management, and to collaborate or compete more effectively to better serve key external customers
- The need to integrate plans of many different kinds—strategic, business, budget, information technology, human resource management, and finance plans, as well as short-term action plans
- Greater difficulty in acquiring the resources they need to fulfill their missions

The leaders and managers of these organizations and communities must think and act strategically, now and in the future, if they are to meet their legal, ethical, and professional obligations successfully. Strategic planning is a must if these organizations are to compete, survive, and prosper and if the "common good" is to be served.

This workbook addresses key issues in the design of an overall strategic planning process and the subsequent implementation process. However, it only touches on the major elements of these processes. We therefore recommend that the workbook be used in tandem with the revised edition of Strategic Planning for Public and Nonprofit Organizations (Bryson, 1995), which places the workbook's guidance and worksheets in a broader context, provides information on other significant issues, reviews relevant details, and alerts users to important caveats.

Furthermore, this workbook is not a substitute for the professional strategic planning consultation and facilitation services that are often needed as part of a strategic planning effort.

Audience

People interested in exploring the applicability of strategic planning to their organizations, networks, or communities
Sponsors, champions, and funders of strategic planning processes
Strategic planning teams
Strategic planning consultants and process facilitators
Teachers and students of strategic planning

Where This Workbook Will Be Relevant

This workbook is designed to be of use to a variety of people and groups:

Organizations as a whole
Parts of organizations (departments, divisions, offices, bureaus, units)
Programs, projects, business processes, and functions (such as personnel, finance, purchasing, information management) that cross departmental lines within an organization
Programs, projects, business processes, and services that involve more than one organization
Networks or groups of organizations
Communities

The worksheets, however, usually assume that the focus of the strategic planning effort is an organization; they will need to be appropriately tailored if the focus is different.

How This Workbook Facilitates Strategic Planning

The strategic planning process is "demystified" and made understandable and accessible.
Fears about the process are allayed through the presentation of a simple, flexible model, step-by-step guidance, and easily understood worksheets.
Process sponsors, champions, consultants, and facilitators are provided with many of the tools they will need to help guide an organization or group through a strategic process of thought and action.
The complex process of strategic planning has been broken down into manageable steps.
The workbook can be used to document progress and keep the process on track.
Communication among process participants is made easier by the workbook's structured approach.

Tangible products emerge from use of the worksheets, including those necessary to develop a strategic plan. These products can help to guide the discussion and the process, and substantiate the need for important changes.

Overview of the Contents

This workbook is divided into two sections:

- Part 1 presents an overview of the strategic planning and implementation process and the benefits to be gained by using it. The chapter on the context and process of strategic change includes five readiness assessment worksheets.
- Part 2 covers each of the ten key steps of the process in more detail. Each step description includes sections on purpose and possible desired planning outcomes, and offers worksheets to facilitate the process.

The book ends with listings of resources, a glossary, and a bibliography.

Acknowledgments

John would like to thank colleagues in Northern Ireland who first saw the possibilities for a strategic planning workbook based on his work and helped him think through what one might look like. He is particularly grateful to the late Jim Maguire for developing and pilot testing an early workbook draft. John is also grateful for the encouragement and efforts of Twila Kirkpatrick, now president of the West Virginia Foundation for Independent Colleges, in pushing the workbook idea further. And he is especially appreciative of Farnum Alston's contributions and his willingness to bring his enormous experience and talent to bear on the workbook project and to see it through to completion. Farnum kept the project alive and took responsibility for most of the preparation and pilot testing of the drafts. Finally, John would like to thank Barbara Crosby for her special insights, constant encouragement, and love throughout the process of developing this workbook.

Farnum would like to express his thanks to many colleagues, clients, and friends who over the years have supported or added their insights to the process of improving public sector governance and thus are a real part of this book: Mark Baughman, William Bechtel, Steve Born, Jerry Bowers, Judith Brown, Tim Farley, Senator Dianne Feinstein, John Gavares, Bryan Gillgrass, Terry Huffman, Scott Hughes, Bud Jordahl, John Kussler, Governor Patrick Lucey, Wally McGuire, Robert O'Neill, Peter Sakai, Dale Stanway, Laurie Thornton, and Michael Wright. Many others also contributed in numerous ways.

Special thanks are due to John Bryson for his collaboration and a friendship that has spanned more than twenty years. His efforts and insight into the need for new public sector and nonprofit tools and methodologies have helped in real ways to improve the quality of service we all receive.

Finally, his deepest gratitude goes to Kirsten Alston, for teaching him the value of love and for providing indispensable professional collaboration and unstinting personal support.

August 1995

John M. Bryson
Minneapolis, Minnesota

Farnum K. Alston
Corte Madera, California

The Authors

John M. Bryson is professor of planning and public affairs at the Hubert H. Humphrey Institute of Public Affairs at the University of Minnesota. He received his B.A. degree (1969) in economics from Cornell University and three degrees from the University of Wisconsin, Madison: his M.A. degree (1972) in public policy and administration, his M.S. degree (1974) in urban and regional planning, and his Ph.D. degree (1978) in urban and regional planning. He is the author of the best-selling *Strategic Planning for Public and Nonprofit Organizations,* now in its second edition (Jossey-Bass, 1995), and of the audiocassette program *Getting Started with Strategic Planning* (Jossey-Bass, 1991). Bryson also coauthored, with Barbara C. Crosby, *Leadership for the Common Good* (Jossey-Bass, 1992), which received the 1993 Terry McAdam Book Award from the Nonprofit Management Association and was named Best Book of 1992–93 by the Public and Nonprofit Sector Division of the Academy of Management.

Bryson is the president of Real-izations, Inc., a Minneapolis-based management consulting firm. He is a past recipient of the General Electric Award for outstanding research in strategic planning from the Academy of Management and has served as a consultant to a wide range of public, nonprofit, and for-profit organizations in North America and Europe.

Farnum K. Alston is founder and president of THE RESOURCES COMPANY (TRC), 21 Sunnyside Avenue, Corte Madera, California, 94925; phone (415) 927-2000; fax (415) 927-1008. TRC is an international consulting firm that specializes in assisting private and public clients with strategic business and technology planning and organizational and management projects. Alston has been conducting such projects for twenty-five years. He received his B.A. degree in economics from the University of California, Berkeley, and did postgraduate work in environmental studies at the University of Wisconsin, Madison. Before founding TRC, he was a partner in KPMG Peat Marwick, San Francisco, where he was also national director of strategic planning and management and director of the firm's economic development practice. He has served in a number of other responsible positions, including deputy mayor and budget director to Mayor (now Senator) Dianne Feinstein, City and County of San Francisco; director of strategic development and senior project manager, Woodward Clyde Consultants, San Francisco; director of the Federal Upper Great Lakes Regional Commission, U.S. Department of Commerce, Washington, D.C.; director of Wisconsin's Upper Great Lakes Regional Commission; and economic development and environmental adviser to Governor Patrick Lucey of Wisconsin. Alston was selected as a charter member of the Federal Senior Executive Service and received an Outstanding Service Award from Juanita Krepps, secretary of the U.S. Department of Commerce.

Creating and Implementing Your Strategic Plan

PART 1

An Overview

Introduction

What Is Strategic Planning?

Strategic planning is "a disciplined effort to produce fundamental decisions and actions that shape and guide what an organization (or other entity) is, what it does, and why it does it" (Bryson, 1995, p. x).

Through strategic planning, public and nonprofit organizations can:

- Examine the environment in which they exist and operate
- Explore the factors and trends that affect the way they do business and carry out their roles
- Seek to meet their mandates and fulfill their missions
- Frame the strategic issues they must address
- Find ways to address these issues by reexamining and reworking organizational mandates and missions, product or service levels and mix, costs and financing, management, or organization

To be effective, strategic planning must be action oriented and must be linked to tactical and operational planning.

The Interactive ABCs of Strategic Planning

Throughout a strategic planning process, there are three fundamental questions that an organization must ask itself (see Figure 1):

A. Who and what are we, what do we do now, and why?
B. What do we want to be and do in the future, and why?
C. How do we get from here to there?

Asking and answering these questions requires an ongoing, iterative conversation among strategic planning team members and other key actors. As the conversation unfolds, new answers to one question can be expected to change previous answers to other questions. The ten-step process and worksheets presented in this workbook provide a reasonable and structured approach to answering the questions.

The Benefits of Strategic Planning

Strategic planning is intended to enhance an organization's ability to think and act strategically. The potential benefits from the process are numerous, although there is no guarantee that they will be realized in practice. These benefits include:

- *Increased effectiveness.* The organization's performance is enhanced, its mission furthered, and its mandates are met. In addition, the organization responds effectively to rapidly changing circumstances.
- *Increased efficiency.* The same or better results are achieved with fewer resources.
- *Improved understanding and better learning.* The organization understands its situation far more clearly. It is able to reconceptualize, if necessary, and to establish an interpretive framework that can guide strategy development and implementation.

Figure 1 ▪ The Interactive ABCs of Strategic Planning

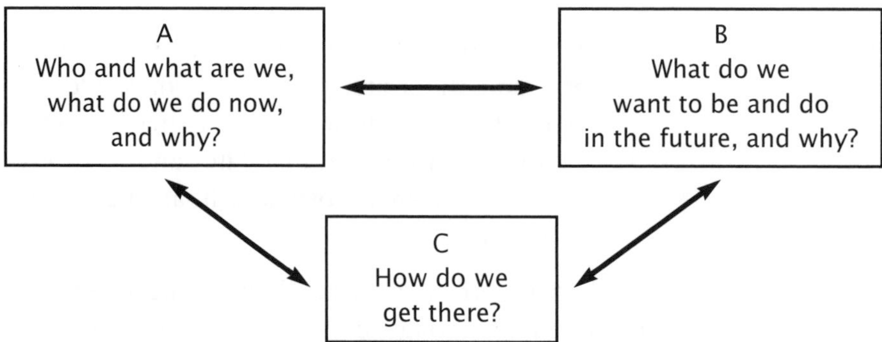

- *Better decision making.* A coherent, focused, and defensible basis for decision making is established, and today's decisions are made in light of their future consequences.
- *Enhanced organizational capabilities.* Broadly based organizational leadership is improved, and the capacity for further strategic thought and action is enhanced.
- *Improved communications and public relations.* Mission, vision, goals, strategies, and action programs are communicated more effectively to key stakeholders. A desirable image for the organization is established and managed.
- *Increased political support.* The organization's legitimacy is enhanced, its advocacy base broadened, and a powerful and supportive coalition developed.

Poor Excuses for Avoiding Strategic Planning

A number of reasons can be offered for not engaging in strategic planning. Too often, however, these "reasons" are actually excuses for avoiding necessary action. For example:

- *We don't have policy board support.* Think strategically about how to gain their support, perhaps for an effort aimed at addressing a single issue.
- *There's no top management support.* Again, think strategically about how to gain their support.
- *Strategic planning won't lead to perfection.* Of course it won't!
- *We're too big (or too small) for strategic planning.* If the U.S. Navy, the Internal Revenue Service, and the smallest nonprofits can benefit from strategic planning—which they do—size is not a legitimate argument for avoiding it.
- *We've got a union.* Then treat the union as another stakeholder.
- *We have personnel policies and individual performance goals to take care of this.* Think strategically about personnel policies and ask whether or not the individual performance goals support desirable organizational strategies.
- *We don't know where to start.* You can start anywhere. The process is so interconnected that you will find yourselves covering most phases through conversation and dialogue no matter where you start.
- *We've already done it—years ago.* Times change. Revisit what you've done to see if it is still relevant.
- *We're perfect already!* Then you *really* need to be careful, because nothing breeds failure like success and the complacency that often comes with it.

Two Legitimate Reasons Not to Undertake Strategic Planning

Strategic planning is not always advisable for an organization. There are two compelling reasons for holding off on a strategic planning effort:

1. Strategic planning may not be the best first step for an organization whose roof has fallen. For example, the organization may need to remedy a cash flow crunch or fill a key leadership position before undertaking strategic planning.
2. If the organization lacks the skills or resources, or the commitment of key decision makers, to carry through an effective strategic planning process and produce a good plan, the effort should not be undertaken. If strategic planning *is* attempted in such a situation, it should probably be a focused and limited effort aimed at developing those skills, resources, and commitments.

The Context and Process of Strategic Change

The Strategy Change Cycle: An Effective Strategic Planning Approach for Public and Nonprofit Organizations

This workbook is organized around a strategic planning and implementation process, the Strategy Change Cycle, which has proved effective for many public and nonprofit organizations. The ten steps of the cycle, presented in Figure 2 on pages 8 and 9, are as follows:

STEP 1 Initiate and Agree on a Strategic Planning Process

The purpose of Step 1 is to negotiate agreement with key internal (and possibly external) decision makers or opinion leaders on the overall strategic planning process, the schedule, and the key planning tasks. Some person or group must initiate the process. One of their first important tasks is to identify the key decision makers. The next is to determine which persons, groups, units, or organizations should be involved in the effort. The initial agreement will be negotiated with at least some of these decision makers, groups, units, or organizations.

Figure 2 ■ The Strategy Change Cycle

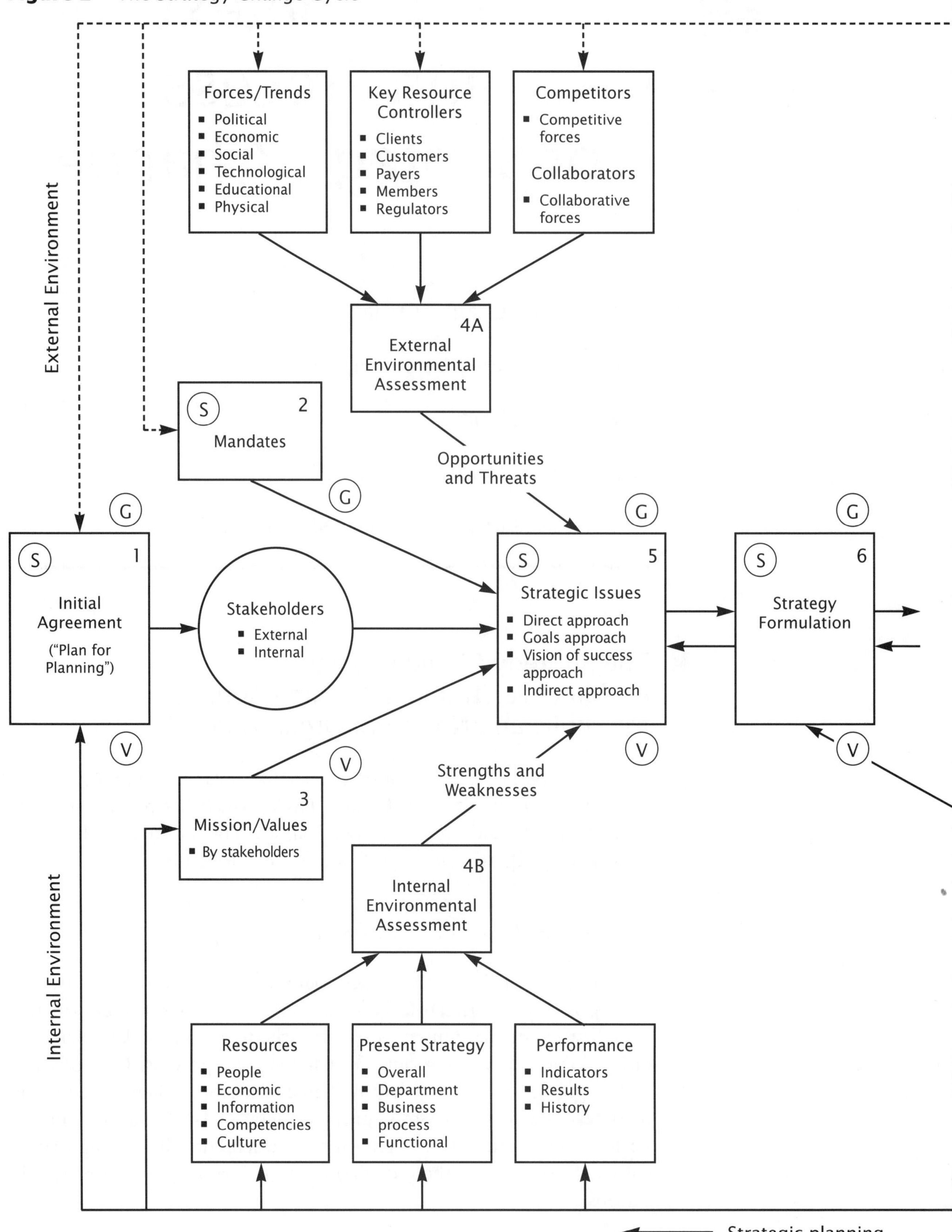

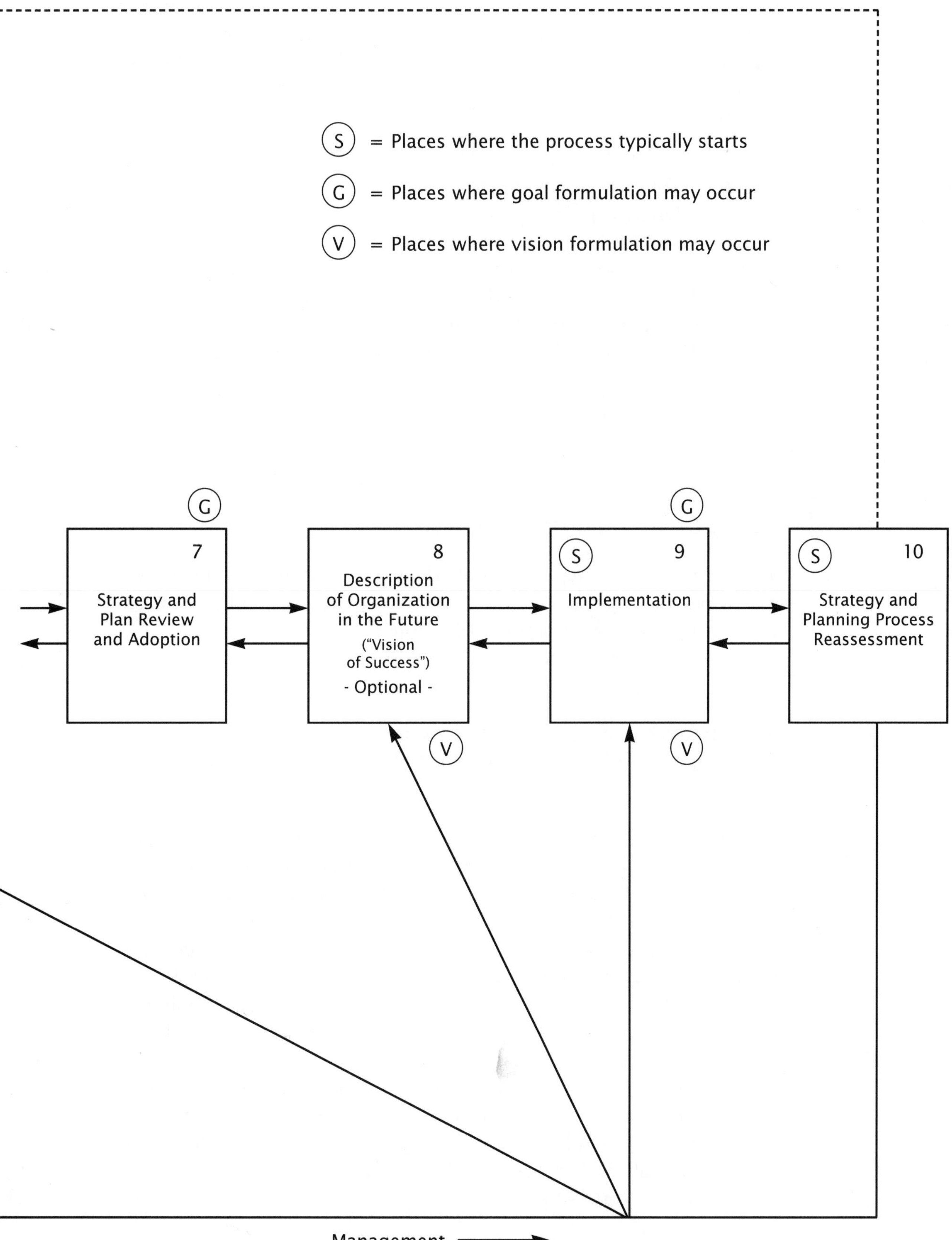
S = Places where the process typically starts
G = Places where goal formulation may occur
V = Places where vision formulation may occur
G
7
Strategy and
Plan Review
and Adoption
8
Description
of Organization
in the Future
("Vision
of Success")
- Optional -
V
G
S
9
Implementation
V
S
10
Strategy and
Planning Process
Reassessment
Management

Before a strategic planning effort is begun, however, it may be useful to perform a readiness assessment. The purpose of such an assessment is to determine how capable the organization is of undertaking a strategic planning effort and whether additional capacity may be needed.

See Worksheets 1–5 at the end of this chapter.

The strategic planning process agreement itself should cover:

- The purpose of the effort
- Preferred steps in the process
- The schedule
- The form and timing of reports
- The role, functions, and membership of any group or committee empowered to oversee the effort
- The role, functions, and membership of the strategic planning team
- Commitment of necessary resources to proceed with the effort

See Worksheet 6.

STEP 2 Clarify Organizational Mandates

The purpose of this step is to clarify the formal and informal mandates placed on the organization (the "musts" it confronts) and to explore their implications for organizational action.

See Worksheets 7 and 8.

STEP 3 Identify and Understand Stakeholders; Develop and Refine Mission and Values

A stakeholder is any person, group, or entity that can place a claim on the organization's attention, resources, or output, or is affected by that output. The key to success for public and nonprofit organizations is the ability to address the needs of crucial stakeholders—according to those stakeholders' criteria.

The organization's mission, in tandem with its mandates, provides its raison d'être. Any government, corporation, agency, or nonprofit organization must seek to meet certain identifiable social or political needs. Viewed in this light, an organization must always be considered the means to an end, not an end in and of itself.

The mission statements developed and refined in this step should grow out of a thorough consideration of who the organization's (or community's) stakeholders are. The organization's value system also might be identified, discussed, and documented.

See Worksheets 9–14.

STEP 4 Assess the Environment to Identify Strengths, Weaknesses, Opportunities, and Threats

In this step, the strengths and weaknesses of the organization are catalogued and evaluated and their strategic implications noted. In addition, the opportunities and threats facing the organization are explored, and again, strategic implications are recognized.

See Worksheets 15–18.

STEP 5 Identify and Frame Strategic Issues

Together, the first four steps of the process lead to the fifth, the identification of strategic issues—the fundamental challenges affecting the organization's mandates, its mission and values, its product or service level and mix, its costs, its financing, its organization, and its management.

See Worksheets 19–22.

STEP 6 Formulate Strategies to Manage the Issues

Strategies are developed to deal with the issues identified in Step 5. Strategies may be of several different types:

- Grand strategy for the organization, network, or community as a whole
- Strategy for organizational subunits
- Program, service, product, or business process strategies
- Strategies, functions such as human resource management, information technology, finance, and purchasing

These strategies can be used to set the context for other change efforts aimed at "reinventing government," "reengineering the organization," "Total Quality Management," "competition or collaboration," and so on.

See Worksheets 23–26.

STEP 7 Review and Adopt the Strategic Plan

The purpose of this step is to gain a formal commitment to adopt and proceed with implementation of the plan(s). This step represents the culmination of the work of the previous steps, and points toward the implementation step in which adopted strategies are realized in practice. Formal adoption may not be necessary in all cases to gain the benefits of strategic planning, but quite often it is.

See Worksheets 27 and 28.

STEP 8 Establish an Effective Organizational Vision for the Future

An organization's "vision of success" outlines what it should look like as it successfully implements its strategies and achieves its full potential. Such a description, to the extent that it is widely known and agreed on in the organization, allows organizational members to know what is expected of them without constant direct managerial oversight. The description also allows other key stakeholders to know what the organization envisions for itself.

Visions of success may be developed at several places in the process, but Step 8 is typically where it happens. Most organizations will not be able to develop an effective vision of success until they have gone through strategic planning more than once. Thus, their visions of success are more likely to serve as a guide for strategy implementation and less as a guide for strategy formulation.

See Worksheet 29.

STEP 9 Develop an Effective Implementation Process

In this step, adopted strategies are implemented throughout the relevant systems. An effective implementation process and action plan must be developed if the strategic plan is to be something other than an organizational New Year's resolution. The more that strategies have been formulated with implementation in mind, and the more active the involvement of those required to implement the plan, the more successful strategy implementation is likely to be.

See Worksheets 30–33.

STEP 10 Reassess Strategies and the Strategic Planning Process

The purpose of the final step is to review implemented strategies and the strategic planning process. The aim is to find out what worked, what did not work, and why, and to set the stage for the next round of strategic planning.

See Worksheets 34 and 35.

The Cycle: Theory Versus Practice

Although the process has been laid out in a linear, sequential manner, it must be emphasized that in practice the process is typically iterative: participants usually rethink what they have done several times before they reach final decisions. Moreover, the process does not always begin at the beginning. Organizations may find themselves confronted with a serious strategic issue or a failing strategy that leads them to engage in strategic planning, and only later do they do Step 1.

It is also important to note that strategic planning efforts necessarily take place within a given context, even if the purpose of the effort is to change the context. Unless strategic planning is being used to design a brand-new organization, it will occur within ongoing processes of organizational change (which are typically cyclical or nonlinear) and must fit those processes. They include budgeting cycles, legislative cycles, decision-making routines of the governing board, and other change initiatives. Among the elements that may be involved are Total Quality Management, information technology, and personnel system reform.

There are also different levels of organizational change, ranging from the more abstract or conceptual (such as changes in mission, vision, and general goals) to the more specific or concrete (such as changes in work plans and budgets). Change may be orchestrated from the top, proceeding "deductively" down to the more concrete and specific level. On the other hand, change may be initiated at the more concrete level and rise, "inductively," toward the more abstract or conceptual level. Most often, change involves a combination of deductive and inductive approaches, and these must be blended as wisely as possible (Mintzberg and Westley, 1992).

It is extremely important to note that, as indicated in Figure 2, goal formulation and visioning activities may be inserted at many points in the process, depending on the circumstances. As often as not, goal formulation comes later in the process, when strategies are formulated. Goals developed there will be reflected in the thrusts of specific strategies. Before that point, any goals that might be agreed on are likely to be too vague to serve as useful guides for action. On the other hand, if agreement can be reached earlier on reasonably specific and detailed goals, they may be used to guide the initial work of the process, to facilitate the framing of strategic issues, or to direct strategy formulation efforts. Similarly, a vision of success typically is developed at the end of the process, to guide implementation, but under certain circumstances may be prepared earlier. As with goals, visioning activities can be used to guide the planning process from the beginning or to frame strategic issues; they can also help in the development of strategies.

Key Design Choices

A number of interconnected design choices must be made to enhance the prospects for a successful strategic planning process. Some of the more important choices are:

- Whose plan is it?
  - Is the plan to be "owned" by a community, organization, organizational unit, program, project, or function?
  - What are the implications of this choice for participation?
- What are the purposes of the strategic planning effort?
  - In what ways are the planning process and the plan intended to enhance organizational or community performance?
  - What other benefits of strategic planning are sought?
  - What values should the process itself embody in the way it is organized and pursued?
- How will the process be tailored to the situation at hand?
  - Has strategic planning been attempted before—successfully or unsuccessfully?
  - Are goal formulation and visioning activities necessary, and if so, where will they occur in the process?
  - Which approach to the identification of strategic issues will be used?
  - How will the process fit with other ongoing organizational processes and change efforts, such as budgeting cycles, or Total Quality Management and information technology initiatives?
- How will the process be managed?
  - Who will sponsor and empower the process?
  - Who will manage the process? Who will the internal process managers—the process champions—be?
  - How will the process be broken down into phases, activities, and tasks?
  - What is the project time frame?
  - What kind of consultation and facilitation will be needed?
  - How will the process accommodate commitments from sponsors and participants in terms of time, energy, and financial and political resources?

What Are the Dangers to Avoid?

There are any number of ways in which strategic planning can fail. Without broad sponsorship, careful and skilled management, adequate resources, excellent timing, and a fair measure of luck, the process may fail. Whenever you ask people to focus in a serious way on what is fundamental and to consider doing things differently, you threaten the existing culture, coalitions, values, and interaction patterns of an organization. Anger, rage, frustration, and rejection of the process may result, no matter how necessary the process may be to ensure organizational survival and prosperity.

There is also an inherent skepticism and resistance to strategic planning among line managers, who have a strong operational orientation—"What will this do for me?"

What Are the Keys to a Successful Process?

In many ways, the keys to success are the mirror image of the potential sources of failure:

Be sure the organization is ready. Conduct a readiness assessment. If the organization is not prepared, identify capacity problems and focus thought and action on remedying them. Use Worksheets 1–5 to assist you in determining whether your organization is ready for strategic planning.

Strengthen leadership and assure adequate participation by key stakeholders. You will need strong sponsors and the support of key stakeholders throughout the process. Include major decision makers, managers, opinion leaders, and other stakeholders essential to the success of the effort.

Build understanding to support wise strategic thought and action. Clearly communicate the purposes of the process to key stakeholders. Engage in the analyses and discussions required to build adequate understanding of the organization, its circumstances, and its potential strategic choices. Manage expectations so that neither too much nor too little is expected of the process. Take the time and allocate the resources to "do it right."

Cultivate necessary political support. Sponsorship by key decision makers is typically crucial to the success of a strategic planning effort. Beyond that, a coalition of supporters must be built that is large enough and strong enough to adopt the strategic plan and support it during implementation.

Foster effective decision making and implementation. Help decision makers focus on the truly important issues. Link the strategic plan to resource allocation decisions. Develop an implementation process and action planning effort that will assure the realization of adopted strategies, and link these processes to operational plans and to resource allocation decisions.

Design a process that is likely to succeed. Build on existing planning, management, and other change efforts and routines, while still keeping the strategic planning process unique and special. Fit the process to the situation at hand. Use the process to inform key decisions. Be realistic about the scope and scale of the strategic planning agenda. Find a way to accommodate the day-to-day demands on people's time. Make sure that people see the process as genuinely helpful.

Manage the process effectively. Commit the resources necessary for a successful effort. Draw on people who are skilled in the process of strategic planning.

Readiness Assessment WORKSHEETS

WORKSHEET 1 Strengths, Weaknesses, Opportunities, Threats

The capacity or "readiness" of an organization to undertake a strategic planning project successfully should be clearly understood by the organization and its project leaders before the process is begun. Organizational barriers to success should be identified and evaluated, and a plan or strategy should be developed to address them. (See Worksheet 2.)

The following organizational areas should be explored through interviews, focus groups, or the use of tailored questionnaires.

I. Mission and Vision

Successful organizations possess a clear understanding of their mandates, and they have established and communicated an inspiring organizational mission and/or vision to their stakeholders.

Please comment below on any significant organizational strengths, weaknesses, opportunities, or threats in the areas of mission and vision. (Use additional space as necessary.)

II. Budget and Human Resource Management

Successful organizations and managers achieve their mandates and fulfill their mission by effectively managing their resources.

Please comment below on any significant organizational strengths, weaknesses, opportunities, or threats in the areas of fiscal and human resources development and management. (Use additional space as necessary.)

III. Communications

Successful organizations have clear, consistent messages and communications networks. *Messages* are concise, they are targeted toward specific stakeholders, and are designed to produce specific responses. *Networks* effectively convey appropriate information to targeted stakeholders, both internal and external.

Please comment on any significant organizational strengths, weaknesses, opportunities, or threats in the area of communications.

IV. Leadership, Management, and Organization

Successful organizations enjoy effective leadership and competent management and organize themselves strategically. *Leadership* means making sure that the organization is doing the right things. *Management* means making sure that those things are being done right. The *organization* should have well-defined relationships horizontally and vertically, which will help it carry out specific strategic initiatives.

Please comment on any significant organizational strengths, weaknesses, opportunities, or threats in the areas of leadership, management, and organization.

WORKSHEET 2 Barriers to Strategic Planning

On the basis of Worksheet 1, what do you see as the *major barriers* to a successful strategic planning process? (*Examples:* lack of leadership; communication problems; resources.) How can they be addressed?

Barriers	Ways They Can Be Addressed

WORKSHEET 3 Expected Costs of Strategic Planning

1. List the costs, direct and/or indirect, you expect to incur from strategic planning. (*Examples:* resources required to implement the process and plan; time required; organizational conflicts and resistance to change; other stakeholder resistance.) Note the most important of these.
2. Note ways to manage these costs.

Costs (direct and indirect)	Ways to Manage Costs

WORKSHEET 4 Expected Benefits of Strategic Planning

1. List the benefits, direct and/or indirect, you expect from strategic planning. (*Examples:* better use of organization's resources; better relations with stakeholders and clients; good plan for change and change management.) Note the most important of these.
2. Note ways to enhance these benefits.

Benefits (direct and indirect)	Ways to Enhance Benefits

WORKSHEET 5 Should We Proceed with the Strategic Planning Process?

Instructions: Review your answers to Worksheets 1 through 4, and determine whether the following readiness criteria have been met. Then discuss results and decide what to do next.

Readiness Criteria

	Yes	No
Process has strong sponsor(s)	☐	☐
Process has strong champion(s)	☐	☐
Resources are available	☐	☐
Process is within our mandate	☐	☐
Benefits outweigh costs	☐	☐
Process will have real value for organization	☐	☐
Process will be linked to operational plans and budget	☐	☐

Based on the above answers, should we

	Yes	No
Proceed	☐	☐
Figure out how to change each no to a yes first	☐	☐
Forget about strategic planning for now	☐	☐

PART 2

Creating and Implementing Strategic Planning: Ten Key Steps

STEP 1

Initiate and Agree on a Strategic Planning Process

Purpose of Step

The purpose of Step 1 is to develop an initial agreement among key decision makers and opinion leaders about the overall strategic planning effort and main planning tasks and to authorize advocates and facilitators to move forward with the process. Certain external decision makers and opinion leaders may need to be parties to the agreement if their support will be essential to the success of the effort.

This initial agreement is one of the most important steps in the whole strategic planning process. In Step 1, many of the commitments necessary to produce a good process and plan are developed. In addition, many critical questions in process design are answered. For example:

- Whose plan is it?
- What are the purposes of the process and plan?
- How will the process be tailored to fit the situation?
- How will the process be managed?
- How will the process be broken down into phases or tasks?
- What schedule will be adopted?

Adequate commitments and wise process design choices are critical to a successful outcome. (Refer to worksheets at the end of this step.)

Possible Desired Planning Outcomes

- Agreement on:

  The worth and scope of the strategic planning effort; organizations, units, groups, or persons who should be involved or informed

Process phases, specific tasks, activities, and schedule
Form and timing of reports

- Formation of a strategic planning coordinating committee (SPCC) that sets process policy and direction
- Formation of a strategic planning team (SPT) that coordinates day-to-day process and plan needs
- Selection of a consultant team of independent process and planning experts to help design and facilitate the process
- Commitment of necessary resources to begin the effort

Worksheet Directions

1. Locate a person or group in your organization or community who will be willing to act as a "process champion"—that is, advocate for strategic planning and initiate the process.
2. Clearly identify "whose" plan it is. Ask your process planning team:
   Who are the process sponsors and the process champions (or champion)?
   What part of the organization (or community) is the plan for? Is it needed? Who will support it? (*Example:* A plan may be a single strategic plan for your whole organization, or it may be a divisional or departmental plan for management only. Both are legitimate if they can address your issues and meet your objectives and expectations.)
3. Make sure that the time frames for the plan and the process are realistic. If they are too long, the plan and the process will not be relevant; if they are too short, the plan will not be strategic and the process will not allow enough time to be strategic. A two-to-five-year plan horizon and a six-to-twelve-month strategic planning process may be reasonable in many cases. Ask your team:
   What information is available, and how reliable is it?
   What issues are driving planning needs? Are they long-term (for example, capital budgeting) or short-term (for example, operations)?
   How rapidly are changes occurring, and what will be the shelf-life of a plan?
4. In planning the process:
   Don't underestimate the level of effort and the time required to do the job well.
   Match the time to the purpose, the process, and the necessary involvements of people in the process.
   Allow adequate time or don't do a strategic plan.

WORKSHEET 6 Profile of the Planning Effort

1. Whose plan is it? The strategic plan is for:

   ☐ The whole organization

   ☐ The whole organization *and* separate plans for major divisions, units, etc.

   ☐ Part of the organization (specify division, unit, program) ________________

   ☐ Other, such as a community interorganizational network (specify) ________________

2. What period will the plan cover?

   ☐ 2 years

   ☐ 5 years

   ☐ 10 years

   ☐ Other (specify) ________________

3. What concerns, problems, or issues do you hope the plan will address?

4. Who is sponsoring the process?

   ☐ Policy board members

   ☐ Senior managers

   ☐ Middle managers

   ☐ Others

5. Who is (are) the process champion(s)?

6. Who will you use on the project team?

   ☐ Policy board members

   ☐ Senior managers

   ☐ Managers

   ☐ Other staff

   ☐ Other stakeholders

   ☐ Consultants

7. What kind and size of team work best in your organization? What does this mean for the composition of a strategic planning team?

8. Who should be involved in the development of the plan?

9. Who should be involved in the review of the plan?

10. How many hours do you wish to give to planning meetings?

    ☐ 1–12

    ☐ 12–24

    ☐ 24–40

    ☐ 40+

11. Are you using consultants or other resource experts?

    ☐ Yes

    ☐ No

    ☐ Unsure

    If unsure, what kind of help do you need?

12. How will you coordinate with and use consultants and process experts?

13. Who will manage the overall planning effort?

14. What type of written plan do you envision?

    ☐ Short executive summary

    ☐ Longer and more detailed but without most tactical and operational elements

    ☐ A detailed plan including tactical and operational elements

    ☐ Other

15. What is the expected time frame for the planning process?

    ☐ 6 months

    ☐ 12 months

    ☐ Other

16. What steps will you use in your planning process? (Review with the people to be involved and refine as needed.)

Steps/Tasks	Persons/Groups Involved	Schedule

Use other sheets as necessary.

17. What resources do you need to complete the effort, and where will you get them?

Source: Adapted from *Strategic Planning Workbook for Nonprofit Organizations,* by Bryan W. Barry. Copyright © 1986 Amherst H. Wilder Foundation, 919 Lafond Avenue, St. Paul, Minnesota, 55104. Used with permission.

STEP 2

Clarify Organizational Mandates

Purpose of Step

The purpose of Step 2 is to clarify the nature and meaning of externally imposed mandates—both formal and informal—that the organization is required to meet. Mandates prescribe what must or should be done under the organization's charter and policies, as well as under federal, state, and local laws, codes, and regulations. In setting a future course for your organization, mandates need to be taken into account as constraints on what you can achieve and how you can achieve it. It is vital that the organization have a clear understanding of its mandates and of their implications for its actions and resources. Many organizations assume that they are far more constrained than they actually are. An equally common error is to overemphasize one aspect of the organization's mandates at the expense of others.

A mandate can be expressed formally or informally, through elections, community expectations, legislation, policy, regulations, procedures, and budget requirements.

Possible Desired Planning Outcomes

- Compilation of the organization's formal and informal mandates
- Interpretation of what is required by the mandates
- Clarification of what is not ruled out by the mandates

Worksheet Directions

1. Have someone compile the formal and informal mandates faced by the organization (Worksheet 7).
2. Review the mandates to clarify what is required and what is allowed. Discuss the implications of the mandates for existing or potential programs, projects, and services and resource allocations. Have individuals fill out Worksheet 8 by themselves first as a basis for getting the discussion started.
3. Frame a clear, concise mandate statement and regularly remind organizational members of what the organization is required to do. This ensures conformity with the mandates and identifies where there is discretionary authority and where there is not. (If mandates are an issue, they may need to be changed.)

WORKSHEET 7 Initial Compilation of Mandates

Mandate	Source (Charter, Policy, Rules, Law, Norms, etc.)	Key Requirements	Effects on Organization	Current Status
				☐ Still Appropriate ☐ Out-of-Date
				☐ Still Appropriate ☐ Out-of-Date
				☐ Still Appropriate ☐ Out-of-Date
				☐ Still Appropriate ☐ Out-of-Date
				☐ Still Appropriate ☐ Out-of-Date
				☐ Still Appropriate ☐ Out-of-Date
				☐ Still Appropriate ☐ Out-of-Date
				☐ Still Appropriate ☐ Out-of-Date
				☐ Still Appropriate ☐ Out-of-Date
				☐ Still Appropriate ☐ Out-of-Date

WORKSHEET 8 Background for Group Discussion of Mandates

Instructions: Individuals should first fill out this worksheet by themselves as a basis for group discussion.

1. Discuss what is "mandated." What does that mean about our purpose and nature as an organization?

2. Discuss the implications of mandates for resource availability and use.

3. Identify programs, services, and product areas *not* ruled out by mandates.

4. Discuss your organization's current mission in relation to its mandates.

5. Discuss mandates that may need to be changed, eliminated, or added.

STEP 3

Identify and Understand Stakeholders; Develop and Refine Mission and Values

Purpose of Step

The key to success for public and nonprofit organizations is satisfying important stakeholders according to each stakeholder's criteria for satisfaction. Mission and values should therefore be thought about in relation to those stakeholders.

Stakeholders

A stakeholder is any person, group, or organization that can place a claim on the organization's resources, attention, or output, or is affected by its output. A stakeholder analysis is the means for identifying who the organization's internal and external stakeholders are, how they evaluate the organization, how they influence the organization, what the organization needs from them, and how important they are. A stakeholder analysis is particularly useful in providing valuable information about the political situation facing the organization.

The results of a stakeholder analysis can form the basis for the development and refinement of a mission statement, but they can also help determine who should be involved in the strategic planning process. (The readiness assessment and Step 1 therefore involved some preliminary stakeholder analysis.) Whom you involve in this process and how you involve them will go a long way toward determining in practice whose process it is and how successful you are likely to be in implementing any plans that are developed.

Mission

In Step 3, the organization's mission is identified, developed, and refined—a process that may also include clarifying the organization's values.

A mission statement is an action-oriented formulation of the organization's reason for existence. The mission statement should be developed in light of who the organization's stakeholders are.

The mission statement for your organization should also serve to define how you propose to get from where you are to where you want to go. It should be meaningful yet concise.

Values

If an organization wants to develop a values statement, the starting point should be the following questions: "How do we want to conduct our business?" "How do we want to treat our key stakeholders?" "What do we value?" An effective values statement process often gives important insight into the organization's goals and strategies.

Possible Desired Planning Outcomes

- An inclusive list of stakeholders and an analysis of how to involve them in the process
- A draft mission statement
- A statement of organizational values

Worksheet Directions

Stakeholders

1. Have your strategic planning team brainstorm a list of key stakeholders (Worksheet 9) and fill out an analysis worksheet for each (Worksheets 10 and 11).
2. On the basis of their analysis, evaluate the involvement of stakeholders in the strategic planning process (Worksheet 12). The plan and the process, if they are to be successful and if they are to be implemented, need to involve and "speak to" key stakeholders. One important area of involvement for both internal and external stakeholders is development of the mission statement.

Mission

1. Identify any existing mission-related materials and have the strategic planning team organize them and fill out Worksheet 13.
2. Have one person or perhaps a small group prepare a draft mission statement. Circulate the draft to stakeholders for their comments. Expect to revisit the mission statement throughout the process.

Values

1. Consider developing an explicit statement of values that indicates how your organization wants to operate and relate to key stakeholders. Values such as respect, trust, and teamwork are often emphasized in such statements. Your statement should articulate a code of behavior to which the organization adheres or aspires.
2. Have your team collect any values-related material and review and discuss it. If there is none, consider developing it through group discussions with your team and key stakeholders. The values discussion can often identify strategic issues. Fill out Worksheet 14.
3. Prepare draft values statements and discuss them. Circulate drafts to key stakeholders for their comments. Expect to revisit values statements throughout the process.

WORKSHEET 9 Stakeholder Identification

External Stakeholders

Internal Stakeholders

WORKSHEET 10 External Stakeholder Analysis

Instructions: An external stakeholder is any person or group outside the organization that can make a claim on the organization's attention, resources, or output or is affected by the organization's output.

For each external stakeholder listed on Worksheet 9, fill out a separate Stakeholder Analysis worksheet.

Rank your stakeholders in terms of their importance to your organization.

Stakeholder:

Criteria Used by Stakeholders to Assess Our Performance	Our Sense of Their Judgment About Our Performance		
	Very Good	Okay	Poor

How do they influence us?

What do we need from them?

How important are they?

- ☐ Extremely
- ☐ Reasonably
- ☐ Not very
- ☐ Not at all

WORKSHEET 11 Internal Stakeholder Analysis

Instructions: An internal stakeholder is any person or group inside the organization that can make a claim on the organization's attention, resources, or output or affects or is affected by the organization's output.

For each internal stakeholder listed on Worksheet 9, fill out a separate Stakeholder Analysis worksheet.

Rank your stakeholders in terms of their importance to your organization.

Stakeholder:

Criteria Used by Stakeholders to Assess Our Performance	Our Sense of Their Judgment About Our Performance		
	Very Good	Okay	Poor

How do they influence us?

What do we need from them?

How important are they?

- ☐ Extremely
- ☐ Reasonably
- ☐ Not very
- ☐ Not at all

WORKSHEET 12 Stakeholder Involvement

Following the analyses on Worksheets 10 and 11, what do you conclude about whether, how, and when to include each stakeholder in the strategic planning process?

Internal Stakeholders

External Stakeholders

WORKSHEET 13 Mission Statement

A mission statement should clarify an organization's purpose and indicate why it is doing what it does. By examining the answers to the following questions, a draft mission statement can be formulated.

1. Who are we? What is our purpose? What business are we in?

2. In general, what are the basic social and political needs we exist to fill? Or: What are the basic social or political problems we exist to address?

3. In general, what do we want to do to recognize or anticipate and respond to these needs or problems?

4. How should we respond to our key stakeholders?

5. What is our philosophy and what are our core values?

6. What makes us distinct or unique?

7. What is our organization's current mission?

8. Is our current mission dated, and if so, how?

9. What changes in the mission would I propose?

10. Examine the answers to the prior questions and draft a mission statement.

WORKSHEET 14 Values Statement

A values statement should identify how an organization conducts itself and what system of values it wishes to operate under, with both internal and external stakeholders.

---

1. List what you consider to be your organization's key values at the present time.

2. What additional values would you like your organization to adopt, to guide the conduct of its business and its relationships with key stakeholders?

3. Having identified both current values and those you would like to see adopted, place an asterisk (*) next to the eight to ten values you consider most important.

4. Drawing on group consensus, develop working definitions of each of these eight to ten values.

5. Now consider how you want to reflect these top values in your strategic plan (for example, as a values list, as broad statements, as part of your vision statement).

STEP 4

Assess the Environment to Identify Strengths, Weaknesses, Opportunities, and Threats

Purpose of Step

In Step 4, internal strengths and weaknesses of the organization are identified, along with the organization's external opportunities and threats. The analysis of these four elements, known by the acronym *SWOT,* is very useful in clarifying the conditions within which the organization operates. While the stakeholder analysis (Step 3) provides extraordinarily useful information about the politics impinging on the organization, the SWOT analysis supplies an overall systems view of the organization and the factors that affect it.

A SWOT analysis provides valuable clues about the probable contours of effective strategies, since every successful strategy builds on strengths and takes advantage of opportunities, while it overcomes or minimizes the effects of weaknesses and threats.

Possible Desired Planning Outcomes

- Lists of internal strengths and weaknesses and external opportunities and threats
- Key background reports
- Specific actions to deal with threats and weaknesses
- Thoughtful discussions among key decision makers concerning strengths, weaknesses, opportunities, and threats and their implications

Worksheet Directions

1. Consider using the snow card technique (see Resources) with the strategic planning team (SPT) to develop an initial list of internal strengths and weaknesses and external opportunities and threats. Fill out Worksheets 15–18.
2. Always try, if possible, to have the SPT consider what is going on *outside* the organization before it considers what is going on *inside.*
3. Encourage the SPT, when it is reviewing its SWOT list, to look for patterns, important actions that might be taken immediately, and implications for the identification of strategic issues.
4. To ensure accuracy and reasonable completeness, conduct a follow-up analysis of the SWOT list developed by the SPT.

WORKSHEET 15 Internal Strengths

Internal strengths are resources or capabilities that help an organization accomplish its mandates or mission. (*Examples:* professional staff, adequate resources, leadership.)

Fill out as many worksheets as are necessary to derive a complete list. Discuss each of the eight to ten strengths you consider of highest priority.

Strength	Description	Options for Keeping or Building on Strength

WORKSHEET 16 Internal Weaknesses

Internal weaknesses are deficiencies in resources and capabilities that hinder an organization's ability to accomplish its mandate or mission. (*Examples:* lack of effective communications, absence of clear vision or mission, flawed organizational structure, noncompetitive pay structure.)

Fill out as many worksheets as are necessary to derive a complete list. Discuss each of the eight to ten weaknesses you consider of highest priority.

Weakness	Description	Options for Minimizing or Overcoming Weakness

WORKSHEET 17 External Opportunities

External opportunities are outside factors or situations that can affect your organization in a favorable way. (*Examples:* new funding from a federal program, political support for a potential project, a chance to modify an outdated mandate.)

Fill out as many worksheets as are necessary to derive a complete list. Discuss the implications for the strategic planning process of the listed opportunities.

Opportunity	Description	Options for Taking Advantage of Opportunity

WORKSHEET 18 External Threats

External threats are outside factors or situations that can affect your organization in a negative way. (*Examples:* loss of state funding, increasing demand for a specific service, union/management conflicts.)

Fill out as many worksheets as are necessary to derive a complete list. Discuss the implications for the strategic planning process of the listed threats.

Threat	Description	Options for Minimizing or Overcoming Threat

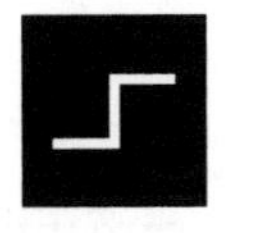

STEP 5
Identify and Frame Strategic Issues

Purpose of Step

A strategic issue is a fundamental challenge affecting an organization's mandates, mission, product or service level and mix, clients or users, costs, financing, organization, or management. The purpose of Step 5 is to identify and frame the fundamental challenges facing the organization.

The identification of strategic issues is the heart of the strategic planning process. The previous steps have been designed to provide information that will help frame the strategic issues in the most constructive way. The manner in which the issues are framed will determine much of the subsequent politics of the process. It will also have a powerful impact on how strategies are formulated, how stakeholders assess their interests and weigh costs and benefits of alternative strategies, and what are likely to be winning and losing arguments in support of various strategies. Issue framing will also directly affect the ease with which the plan can be implemented.

Issues fall into three main categories:

- Current issues that probably require immediate action
- Issues on the horizon that are likely to require action in the near future
- Issues for which it is unclear whether any action will be required now or in the future, but that need to be monitored

Possible Desired Planning Outcomes

- An inclusive list of strategic issues faced by the organization
- An ordering of the issues in terms of priority or some other relevant classification.

Worksheet Directions

1. Have individual members of the strategic planning team fill out Worksheet 19, using one copy of the worksheet for each of five to nine possible issues.
2. Compare the individual responses given on Worksheet 19. Fill out Worksheet 20 as a team.
3. Have the strategic planning team develop a master strategic issue statement for each issue, using Worksheet 21.
4. Decide if each issue is operational or strategic by using Worksheet 22. There is no absolute test to establish whether an issue is strategic or operational. There is a large gray area into which many issues will fall and the assessment of their strategic importance is a judgment that must be made by policy makers or top management. To assist leaders and managers in making this judgment, the questionnaire in Worksheet 22 may be applied to each issue. Generally speaking, major strategic issues will be characterized by answers that fall predominantly in columns two and three. Operational issues will tend to be characterized by answers that fall predominantly in columns one and two.
5. Decide on priorities among key issues. Consider using the "dot technique" for prioritizing: Each member of the strategic planning team gets five to seven colored stick-on dots, numbered in sequence from one. He or she may "vote" for an issue by placing a dot next to it, the higher numbers reflecting higher priorities. When everyone has thus indicated what they feel are the most important strategic issues facing the organization, the weighted votes are tallied. The issues with the highest number of points then become the key issues for consideration in the strategic planning process.
6. Develop new master worksheets (Worksheet 20), if necessary, for the key issues. Consider what the organization's goals might be in addressing each issue. Also remember that every strategic issue involves some form of conflict. Among the questions to be struggled over are:
   What will be done?
   How will it be done?
   When will it be done?
   Who will do it?
   Who will benefit by it and who will not?

WORKSHEET 19 Individual Strategic Issue Identification

Instructions: The purpose of identifying selected strategic issues is to enable the organization to focus on key challenges or policy choices. This worksheet is to be filled out by individuals.

Complete a separate worksheet for each of five to nine issues.

1. What is the issue? Be sure to phrase the issue as a question that has more than one answer. The issue should be one the organization can do something about.

2. Why is this an issue? How is it related to the organization's mission, mandates, internal strengths and weaknesses, or external opportunities and threats?

   Mission

   Mandates

Strengths

Weaknesses

Opportunities

Threats

3. What are the consequences of not addressing this issue?

WORKSHEET 20 Master List of Key Issues

Instructions: Prepare a master list of key issues phrased as questions that have more than one answer. The issues should be ones the organization can do something about.

1.

2.

3.

4.

5.

6.

7.

8.

9.

10.

11.

12.

13.

14.

15.

16.

17.

18.

19.

20.

WORKSHEET 21 Master Strategic Issues Statement

Instructions: The master list of key issues identifies the major challenges that are likely to be the focus of the rest of the strategic planning effort. Fill out a separate worksheet for each issue on the Master List of Key Issues (Worksheet 20).

1. What is the issue? Be sure to phrase the issue as a question that has more than one answer. The issue should be one the organization can do something about.

2. Why is this an issue? How is it related to the organization's mission, mandates, internal strengths and weaknesses, or external opportunities and threats?

   Mission

   Mandates

Strengths

Weaknesses

Opportunities

Threats

3. What are the consequences of not addressing this issue?

4. What should our goals be in addressing this issue?

WORKSHEET 22 Operational Versus Strategic Issues

Issue: Issue is: ☐ Primarily operational ☐ Primarily strategic

	Operational ◄──		──► Strategic
1. Is the issue on the agenda of the organization's policy board (whether elected or appointed)?	No		Yes
2. Is the issue on the agenda of the organization's chief executive (whether elected or appointed)?	No		Yes
3. When will the strategic issues' challenge or opportunity confront you?	Right now	Next year	Two or more years from now
4. How broad an impact will the issue have?	Single unit or division		Entire organization
5. How large is your organization's financial risk/opportunity?	Minor (≤10% of budget)	Moderate (10–15% of budget)	Major (≥25% of budget)
6. Will strategies for issue resolution likely require: a. Development of new service goals and programs?	No		Yes
b. Significant changes in revenue sources or amounts?	No		Yes
c. Significant amendments in federal or state statutes or regulations?	No		Yes
d. Major facility additions or modifications?	No		Yes
e. Significant staff expansion?	No		Yes
7. How apparent is the best approach for issue resolution?	Obvious, ready to implement	Broad parameters, few details	Wide open
8. What is the lowest level of management that can decide how to deal with this issue?	Line staff supervisor		Head of major department
9. What are the probable consequences of not addressing this issue?	Inconvenience, inefficiency	Significant service disruption, financial losses	Major long-term service disruption and large cost/revenue setbacks
10. How many other groups are affected by this issue and must be involved in resolution?	None	1–3	4 or more
11. How sensitive or "charged" is the issue relative to community, social, political, religious, and cultural values?	Benign	Touchy	Dynamite

Source: Adapted from Hennepin County Office of Planning and Development, 1983, pp. 2–6.

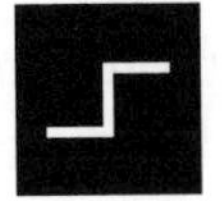

STEP 6
Formulate Strategies to Manage the Issues

■ Purpose of Step

The purpose of Step 6 is to create a set of strategies to address each issue that has been identified in Step 5, so that the organization can better fulfill its mission, meet its mandates, and achieve its issue-specific goals.

Strategy is a *pattern* of purposes, policies, programs, projects, actions, decisions, and resource allocations that defines what an organization is, what it does, and why it does it. Strategies can vary by level, function, and time frame.

■ Possible Desired Planning Outcomes

- Preparation of strategy statements of different kinds:
  - Grand strategy for the organization as a whole
  - Division or subunit strategy statements
  - Program, service, product, project, or business process strategies
  - Strategy statements for specific functions, such as human resources management, finance, and information technology
- Preparation of draft strategic plans
- Actions taken when they are identified and become useful or necessary

■ Worksheet Directions for Strategy Development

1. Remember that what is important is strategic thinking and acting, not the particular approach to strategy formulation or the develop-

ment of a formal strategic plan. Step 6 is likely to be more interactive than previous steps because of the need to find the best fit among strategies and among elements of each strategy.

2. Develop answers to the five questions on Worksheet 23 (Spencer, 1989), which may be filled out by boards, the strategic planning team (SPT), task forces, operational managers and selected staff, or others. The same people do not have to answer all five questions. The strategic planning coordinating committee or the SPT may tackle the first three, for example, while other work groups may be assigned the task of answering the next two. In some circumstances, answering the last two questions may be postponed until after Step 7 (Review and Adopt the Strategic Plan) has been completed.
3. Have the SPT organize the Worksheet 23 responses into coherent sets of strategies, showing how the strategies address particular issues or achieve issue-specific goals and identifying the parts of the organization that would be required to implement the strategies. (Use Worksheet 24.)
4. Make sure that strategies are described in reasonable detail, to allow informed judgments to be made about their efficacy and to provide reasonable guidance for assessing the implications for implementation and for the organization in general.
5. Ask the SPT to establish criteria for the evaluation of each suggested strategy. (Use Worksheet 25, one copy of which should be filled out for each strategy.)
6. Allow for consultation between the SPT and key stakeholders, so that the planning team can determine priorities among strategies for each issue or issue-related goal.
7. Develop a final strategy statement for each strategy, based on Worksheet 24.
8. Encourage the strategic planning team to develop a draft strategic plan. Information may be drawn from prior worksheets, and Worksheet 26 may be used as a checklist for a model for the plan.

Worksheet Directions for Plan Development

1. Even if a formal strategic plan is not prepared, consider developing a set of interrelated strategy statements describing:
   - Grand strategy
   - Organizational subunit strategies
   - Program, service, product, project, or business strategies
   - Functional strategies

2. Employ a structured process to review strategy statements and formal strategic plans. Review sessions may be structured around the following agenda:
   Overview of plan
   General discussion of plan and reactions to it
   Brainstorming of plan strengths and weaknesses
   Brainstorming of plan opportunities and threats
   Brainstorming of modifications that would improve on strengths and opportunities and minimize or overcome weaknesses and threats
   Agreement on next steps to complete the plan

WORKSHEET 23 Five Key Questions for Identifying Strategies

Instructions: Fill out a separate worksheet for each issue.

Strategic issue:

Issue-specific goals:

1. What are the practical alternatives, dreams, or visions we might pursue to address this issue and achieve our goal?

2. What are the barriers to realizing these alternatives, dreams, or visions?

3. What major initiatives might we pursue to achieve these alternatives, dreams, or visions directly, or else indirectly through overcoming the barriers?

4. What are the key actions (with existing resources of people and dollars) that must be taken this year to implement the major initiatives?

5. What specific steps must be taken within the next six months to implement the major initiatives, and who is responsible for taking them?

Step	Party responsible for step

WORKSHEET 24 Strategy Statement

1. What is the purpose of the strategy?

2. What are the strategy's key elements?

3. How does the strategy address the issue and achieve issue-specific goals?

4. What parts of the organization are required to implement the strategy?

   ☐ Whole Organization

   ☐ Department(s)

   ☐ Division(s)

   ☐ Unit(s)/Function(s)

WORKSHEET 25 Checklist of Suggested Criteria for Evaluating Strategies

Instructions: Identify the issue and goals to be addressed, and the performance measures to be used. Evaluate how well the strategy performs against the following criteria:

Issue:

Strategy:

Goals:

Objectives:

Performance measures:

Acceptability to key decision makers, stakeholders, and opinion leaders

Acceptability to the general public

Client or user impact

Relevance to the issue

Consistency with mission, values, philosophy, and culture

Coordination or integration with other strategies, programs, and activities

Technical feasibility

Cost and financing

Cost-effectiveness

Long-term impact

Risk assessment

Staff requirements

Flexibility or adaptability

Timing

Facility requirements

Other appropriate criteria

WORKSHEET 26 Checklist for the Strategic Plan Model

Strategic plans vary in their content and design. The following elements might be included.

Element	See Worksheet(s):	Include Yes	Include No
☐ Introduction Purpose Process Participation	6		
☐ Mission statement	13		
☐ Values statement	14		
☐ Vision statement	29		
☐ Mandates	7, 8		
☐ Environmental analysis, including SWOT analysis	15, 16, 17, 18		
☐ Strategic issues or challenges	19, 20, 21		
☐ Grand strategy statement	23, 24, 25		
☐ Goals, objectives, and performance measures	7, 8, 10, 11, 13, 14, 21, 23, 24, 25, 29		
☐ Issue-specific strategies	23, 24		
☐ Subunit strategy statements	23, 24		
☐ Program, service, product, or business process plans	23, 24		
☐ Functional strategy statements	23, 24		
☐ Staffing plans	23, 24, 30, 31, 32, 33		
☐ Financial plans	23, 24, 30, 31, 32, 33		
☐ Implementation and action plans	23, 24, 30, 31, 32, 33		
☐ Monitoring and evaluation plans	23, 24, 25, 33, 34, 35		
☐ Plans for updating all or part of the plan	33, 34, 35		

STEP 7
Review and Adopt the Strategic Plan

Purpose of Step

The purpose of Step 7 is to reach an official organizational decision to adopt and proceed with the strategic plan or plans. This step may merge with Step 6 (Formulate Strategies to Manage the Issues) in a single organization. But a separate step is likely to be necessary when strategic planning is undertaken for a community or network of organizations. The strategic planning coordinating committee (SPCC) will need to adopt the plan, and implementing organizations will also need to adopt it—or at least parts of it—in order for implementation to proceed effectively.

Possible Desired Planning Outcomes

- Widely shared agreement on the strategic plan among key decision makers and a decision to adopt it and proceed with implementation
- Provision of the necessary guidance and resources for implementation
- Substantial support from those who can strongly affect implementation success
- Widely shared sense of excitement about the substance and symbolism of the plan

Worksheet Directions

1. Determine who needs to be involved in reviewing and adopting the strategic plan. (Use Worksheet 27.)

Continue to pay attention to the goals, concerns, and interests of all key stakeholders.

Obtain necessary resource commitments, if at all possible, prior to the formal adoption session.

Remember that incentives must reward behavior that will lead to effective implementation.

Assess the nature and strength of supporting and opposing coalitions.

Build support for the plan.

Identify one or more sponsors and champions to gain passage in the relevant arenas.

2. Have your team assess how best to reach key stakeholders.

   Reduce decision-maker uncertainty about the proposed plan.

   Develop arguments and counterarguments in support of the proposal prior to formal review sessions.

   Engage formal review bodies in structured review sessions that focus on proposal strengths, weaknesses, and modifications. (Use Worksheet 28.)

   Remember that some people or groups may not want the plan to be adopted or implemented.

3. Appoint a lead person or small team to produce the actual plan (if one is not already prepared), and obtain the necessary reviews.

   Be prepared to bargain and negotiate over proposal features or other issues in exchange for support. This is part of the process.

   Provide a "public" announcement of the plan, at least within the organization and for key stakeholders.

WORKSHEET 27 Plan Review and Adoption Process

1. Determine who needs to participate in reviewing and adopting the plan.

Plan Review	Plan Adoption

2. Assess who will support or oppose the plan.

Support	Opposition

3. What could be done to maintain support and to convert opposition to support?

4. Develop a plan review and adoption process.

What Will Be Done	Who Will Do It	When It Will Be Done	How It Will Be Done

5. Outline a communications and information process to inform key stakeholders of the plan, the review process, and its adoption. (*Examples:* memos, newsletters, meetings, focus groups.)

6. Identify resources necessary for implementation of the strategic plan and indicate whether or not they are assured.

	Assured	
	Yes	No

WORKSHEET 28 Plan Evaluation

Strengths

Weaknesses

Modifications That Would Improve the Plan

STEP 8

Establish an Effective Organizational Vision for the Future

Purpose of Step

In Step 8, an organizational "vision of success" is prepared, describing what the organization should look like as it successfully implements its strategies and achieves its full potential. An organization typically has to go through more than one cycle of strategic planning before it can develop an effective vision for itself. A vision of success is therefore more likely to be a guide to strategy implementation than strategy formulation.

All that is really necessary to enhance organizational achievement is to identify a few key issues and to do something effective about them. Nonetheless, if a vision of success can be prepared, it should be. Such a vision can be extremely important for educational purposes and for allowing constructive action to be taken anywhere in the organization without constant oversight by leaders and managers.

Possible Desired Planning Outcomes

- Preparation of a short and inspiring "vision of success"
- Wide circulation of the vision among organizational members and other key stakeholders after appropriate consultations, reviews, and sign-offs
- Use of the vision to influence major and minor organizational decisions and actions

Worksheet Directions

1. Have your team collect any vision-related materials and documents. Review and discuss these, then consider developing a vision statement

through group discussions with your team and key stakeholders. Many of the elements of a vision of success will have been described in the course of the strategic planning process. A vision of success should include the following information about an organization:

Mission
Basic philosophy and core values
Basic strategies
Performance criteria
Major decision rules
Ethical standards applied to all employees

2. Have your team or key stakeholder representatives break into small groups and individually fill out Worksheet 29. The group should then share and discuss their answers.
3. Following the discussion, request that someone prepare a draft vision statement.
4. Circulate drafts to key stakeholders for their comments and make modifications as appropriate until general agreement is reached.
5. Communicate your organization's vision statement to key stakeholders, both internal and external.
6. Expect to revisit the vision statement throughout the process and in the future. It will change as the organization and the factors affecting the organization change.

WORKSHEET 29 Vision of Success

1. What is the organization's mission? (See Worksheet 13.)

2. What are the organization's basic philosophies and core values? (See Worksheet 14.)

3. What are its basic strategies? (See Worksheet 24.)

4. What are its performance criteria? (See Worksheets 7, 8, 10, 11, 13, 14, 21, 23, 24, 25, and 29.)

5. What are the major decision rules followed by the organization?

- What processes and procedures are followed to make major decisions? To make minor decisions?

- What is decided centrally?

- What is delegated?

- How are exceptions handled?

6. What ethical standards are expected of all employees?

7. Draft a vision statement for your organization, based on your answers to the first six questions.

STEP 9

Develop an Effective Implementation Process

Purpose of Step

The purpose of Step 9 is to incorporate adopted strategies throughout the relevant systems. The mere creation of a strategic plan is not enough. Developing an effective action plan and implementation process will bring life to the strategies and create real value for the organization and its stakeholders.

Possible Desired Planning Outcomes

- Real *value added* through goal achievement and heightened stakeholder satisfaction
- Clear understanding of what needs to be done, by whom, when, and why
- Reasonably smooth and rapid introduction of the strategies throughout the relevant systems; adoption of the changes by all relevant organizations, units, groups, and individuals in a timely fashion
- Development of a widely shared "vision of success" to guide implementation (if one was not developed earlier)
- Use of a "debugging" process to identify and fix difficulties that almost inevitably arise as a new strategy is put into place
- Use of a formal evaluation process to determine if substantive and symbolic strategic goals have been achieved
- Assurance that important features of the strategy are maintained throughout the implementation process
- Establishment of, or provision for, review points at which maintenance, replacement, or termination of the strategies can be considered

- Timely updating of the strategic plan and relevant implementation plans

Worksheet Directions

1. Think strategically about implementation. Consciously manage implementation so that important public and nonprofit purposes are furthered.
2. Clearly document your organization's existing programs, services, and projects, using Worksheet 30. An understanding of what the organization is currently doing is the starting point for the effective integration of the strategic planning priorities. The organization will need to shift some or all of its efforts and resources to the higher-level priorities reflected in the strategic plan.
3. Using Worksheet 31, document the strategic plan's program, service, and project impacts. Then use Worksheet 32 to reconcile the organization's current activities with those envisioned in the strategic plan.
4. For each strategy that has been developed through the strategic planning process, develop a clearly defined action plan (Worksheet 33) that answers the who, what, and when questions. Involve the operations and administrative stakeholders in this key step. (A phased approach to the implementation of the strategic plan may be necessary, given the organization's resource situation and its mandates.) Action plans, which must be carefully coordinated, should detail:
   Specific expected results, objectives, and milestones
   Roles and responsibilities of implementation bodies, teams, and individuals
   Specific action steps
   Schedules
   Resource requirements and sources
   A communication process
   A review and monitoring process
   Accountability processes and procedures
5. If necessary for effective follow-through, replace the strategic planning team with an implementation planning team whose membership may be different.

WORKSHEET 30 Existing Programs, Services, and Projects: Evaluation

Existing Programs, Services, Projects	Criteria for Priority	Priority (Low/ Moderate/ High)	Client and Organization Impact	Resources Used		
				People	$	Time Frame

WORKSHEET 31 Strategic Plan's Proposed Programs, Services, and Projects: Evaluation

Proposed Programs, Services, Projects	Criteria for Priority	Priority (Low/ Moderate/ High)	Client and Organization Impact	Resources Used		
				People	$	Time Frame

WORKSHEET 32 Prioritizing Programs, Services, and Projects

Instructions: Using Worksheets 30 and 31, compile a master list of priorities that reconciles the organization's current programs, services, and projects with those proposed in the strategic plan.

Existing Priorities That Should Be Retained (Programs, Services, Projects)	Strategic Plan Priorities That Should Be Pursued (Programs, Services, Projects)

WORKSHEET 33 Action Planning

Instructions: For each priority listed on Worksheet 32, explore the following aspects of an action plan:

Priority:

Relevant strategy:

1. What specific actions must be taken to implement the strategy in the next six months to a year?

2. What are the expected results and milestones?

3. Who are the responsible parties? What are their roles and responsibilities?

4. When will the actions be taken?

5. What resources will be required and where will they be obtained?

6. How will action plan implementation be reviewed and monitored and accountability assured?

STEP 10

Reassess Strategies and the Strategic Planning Process

Purpose of Step

The purpose of this final step is to review implemented strategies and the strategic planning process as a prelude to a new round of strategic planning. Much of the work of this phase may occur as part of the ongoing implementation process. However, if an organization has not engaged in strategic planning for a while, it may be useful to mark off this step as a separate one.

In this step, an effort is made to reassess strategies in order to decide what should be done about them. Strategies may need to be maintained, superseded by other strategies, or terminated for one reason or another. An attempt is also made in this step to figure out whether a new round of strategic planning is warranted.

Possible Desired Planning Outcomes

- Assurance that implemented strategies remain responsive to real needs and problems—and if they don't, consideration of what should be done with them
- Resolution of residual problems that become evident during sustained implementation
- Clarification of the strengths and weaknesses of the most recent strategic planning effort, and discussion of modifications that might be made in the next round of strategic planning
- Development of the energy, will, and ideas necessary to revise existing strategies, address important unresolved strategic issues, or undertake a full-blown strategic planning exercise

Worksheet Directions

1. At some point after implementation of the strategic plan has begun, evaluate not only the plan but the strategic planning process itself.
2. Strategy implementation is an ongoing process, not a one-time event, and the most effective way to improve it is to evaluate the success of prior efforts. Consider who should be involved in this effort (for example, key stakeholders, outside experts, strategic planning team, implementers). (Use Worksheet 34.)
3. On the basis of the evaluation and its findings, decide if a new round of strategic plans is needed and what changes might be indicated. If a new round is thought necessary, fill out Worksheet 35 as a first step in charting possible improvements.

WORKSHEET 34 Improving Existing Strategies

Strategy	Strengths	Weaknesses	Modifications That Would Improve	Summary Evaluation
				☐ Maintain ☐ Replace with a new or revised element ☐ Terminate
				☐ Maintain ☐ Replace with a new or revised element ☐ Terminate
				☐ Maintain ☐ Replace with a new or revised element ☐ Terminate
				☐ Maintain ☐ Replace with a new or revised element ☐ Terminate
				☐ Maintain ☐ Replace with a new or revised element ☐ Terminate

WORKSHEET 35 Improving the Strategic Planning Process

Planning Process Element	Strengths	Weaknesses	Modifications That Would Improve	Summary Evaluation
				☐ Maintain ☐ Replace with a new or revised element ☐ Terminate
				☐ Maintain ☐ Replace with a new or revised element ☐ Terminate
				☐ Maintain ☐ Replace with a new or revised element ☐ Terminate
				☐ Maintain ☐ Replace with a new or revised element ☐ Terminate
				☐ Maintain ☐ Replace with a new or revised element ☐ Terminate

Resources

A. Brainstorming Guidelines

B. Snow Card Guidelines

C. Strategic Planning Workshop Equipment Checklist

D. Conference Room Setup Checklist

A. Brainstorming Guidelines

1. Agree to participate in a brainstorming exercise.
2. Do not criticize or evaluate any of the ideas that are put forward; they are simply placed before the group and recorded.
3. Be open to hearing some wild ideas in the spontaneity that evolves when the group suspends judgment. Practical considerations are not important at this point. The session is freewheeling.
4. Emphasize that the quantity of ideas counts, not their quality. All ideas should be expressed, and none should be screened out by any participant. A great number of ideas will increase the likelihood of the group discovering good ones.
5. Build on the ideas of other group members when possible. Pool your creativity. Everyone should be free to build onto ideas and to make interesting amalgams from the various suggestions.
6. Focus on a *single* problem or issue. Don't skip around to various problems or try to brainstorm answers to a complex, multiple problem.
7. Foster a congenial, relaxed, cooperative atmosphere.
8. Make sure that all members, no matter how shy and reluctant to contribute, get their ideas heard.
9. Record *all* ideas.

B. Snow Card Guidelines

1. Bring a single problem or issue into the group.
2. Have individuals in the group brainstorm as many ideas as possible and record them on individual worksheets.
3. Ask individuals to pick out their five "best items" and transcribe each one onto its own "snow card"—half of an 8½-inch by 11-inch sheet of paper, a 5- by 7-inch card, or a large Post-it note.
4. Shuffle the cards, then tape them to a wall in categories. The group should determine the categories after reviewing several of the items. The resulting clusters of cards may resemble a "blizzard" of ideas–hence the term *snow cards.*
5. Establish subcategories as needed.
6. Once all items are on the wall and included in a category, rearrange and tinker with the categories until they make the most sense.
7. When finished, take down the cards in their categories and have all the ideas typed up and distributed to the group.

Source: These guidelines are based on a technique developed by Richard B. Duke of the University of Michigan and by the Institute for Cultural Affairs (Spencer, 1989).

C. Strategic Planning Workshop Equipment Checklist

____ Strategic planning process outlines

____ Strategic planning workbooks *(Creating and Implementing Your Strategic Plan)*

____ Strategic planning books (Bryson, 1995)

____ Strategic planning videos

____ Sample strategic plans

____ Snow cards (35 per person) (see Resource B)

____ Broad-tipped marking pens for snow cards (dark colors)

____ Flip charts and easels (two or more)

____ Broad-tipped marking pens for flip charts and whiteboards (various colors)

____ Masking tape

____ Drafting tape

____ Stick-on dots in different colors

____ Post-it notes

____ Overhead projector (including spare bulb)

____ Blank transparencies

____ Nonpermanent marking pens for transparencies

____ Screen

____ Slide projector

____ Video monitor

____ VCR

____ Audiotape player

____ Extension cords

____ Still camera, film, and flash attachment

____ Access to one-hour photo shop

____ Access to computer and printer

____ Access to photocopy machine

____ Secretarial support

D. Conference Room Setup Checklist

____ Good lighting and ventilation

____ Comfortable setting, free of distractions and phones

____ Small tables that can be moved out of the way

____ Comfortable, movable chairs

____ Adequate breakout area(s)

____ Walls to which flip charts or snow cards can be taped

____ Adequate electrical outlets

____ Coffee/tea/soft drinks/mineral water

____ Bread/rolls

____ Fresh fruit

____ Hard candies

Glossary

Action plan A plan for the day-to-day operation of a business over the next one to twelve months. It includes a prioritized list of proposed projects as well as plans for all projects that have been funded. Development of an action plan requires no more than two months. The action plan should be reviewed and updated weekly.

Goal A long-term organizational target or direction of development. It states what the organization wants to accomplish or become over the next several years. Goals provide the basis for decisions about the nature, scope, and relative priorities of all projects and activities. Everything the organization does should help it move toward attainment of one or more goals.

Milestone A significant date or event during execution of a project—often associated with the end of a phase or subphase.

Mission statement A statement of organizational purpose.

Objective A measurable target that must be met on the way to attaining a goal.

Performance measure A means of objectively assessing the results of programs, products, projects, or services.

Stakeholder Any person, group, or organization that can place a claim on an organization's attention, resources, or output, or is affected by that output.

Strategic planning A disciplined effort to produce fundamental decisions and actions that shape and guide what an organization is, what it does, and why it does it.

Strategy The means by which an organization intends to accomplish a goal or objective. It summarizes a pattern across policies, programs, projects, actions, decisions, and resource allocations.

Values statement A description of the code of behavior (in relation to employees, other key stakeholders, and society at large) to which an organization adheres or aspires.

Vision statement A description of what an organization will look like if it succeeds in implementing its strategies and achieves its full potential.

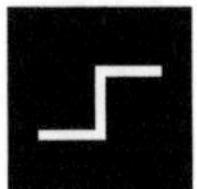

Bibliography

Barry, B. W. *Strategic Planning Workbook for Nonprofit Organizations.* Saint Paul, Minn.: Amherst H. Wilder Foundation, 1986.

Bryson, J. M. *Strategic Planning for Public and Nonprofit Organizations.* (Rev. ed.) San Francisco: Jossey-Bass, 1995.

Bryson, J. M., and Crosby, B. C. *Leadership for the Common Good: Tackling Public Problems in a Shared-Power World.* San Francisco: Jossey-Bass, 1992.

Hennepin County Office of Planning and Development. *Strategic Planning Manual.* Minneapolis: Office of Planning and Development, Hennepin County, Minn., 1983.

Johnson, D. W., and Johnson, F. P. *Joining Together: Group Theory and Group Skills.* (5th ed.) Englewood Cliffs, N.J.: Prentice Hall, 1994.

Mintzberg, H., and Westley, F. "Cycles of Organizational Change," *Strategic Management Journal,* 1992, *13,* 39–59.

Nutt, P. C., and Backoff, R. W. *Strategic Management of Public and Third Sector Organizations: A Handbook for Leaders.* San Francisco: Jossey-Bass, 1992.

Schwarz, R. M. *The Skilled Facilitator: Practical Wisdom for Developing Effective Groups.* San Francisco: Jossey-Bass, 1994.

Spencer, L. *Winning Through Participation.* Dubuque, Iowa: Kendall/Hunt, 1989.